LET'S EXPLORE SCIENCE

Restoring Wetlands

AUTHOR
JEANNE STURM

ROURKE PUBLISHING
Vero Beach, Florida 32964

www.rourkepublishing.com

PHOTO CREDITS: © Diane Labombarbe: 3; © Jitalia17: 4; © USDA: 5; © Terry Healy: 6, 7; © Ann Taylor-Hughes: 8; © Mike Norton: 9; © oneclearvision: 10; © Daniel Bobrowsky: 10; © Chet Mitchell: 11; © James Gritz: 11; © Kevin Woodrow: 11; © John Anderson: 12, 45; © Michael Ray: 13, 14, 25, 41; © john miller: 13; © Alexander Hafemann: 14, 15; © William Mahar: 15; © Stephanie Tomlinson: 15; © Janusz Gniadek: 16; © fotoIE: 16; © Kevin Snair: 17; © jamesbenet: 18; © Michael Pettigrew: 19; © Wikipedia: 19; © Ruth Peterkin: 20; © Andriy Adrov: 20; © John Pitcher: 21; © Brian Sak: 22; © Pauline S. Mill: 23; © JMWScout: 23; © fotoVoyager: 26, 27, 30, 31, 34, 35, 38, 39, 42, 43, 46, 47, 24, 25nm; © William Hopkins: 26; © Wikipedia: 27; © Eric Isselée: 28; © Jim Jurica: 29; © Associated Press: 30, 40; © Stephan Sweet: 31; © Bart Coenders: 32; © Tomasz Szymanski: 32; © Karen Massier: 33; © Jorge Delgado: 34; © Victor Polyakov: 35; © Hugo de Wolf: 36, 37; © Susan Traynor: 40; © pamspix: 39; © roccomontoya: 41; © Jordan Roderick: 43; © Fish and Wildlife Service: 44

Edited by Kelli L. Hicks

Cover and Interior design by Teri Intzegian

Library of Congress Cataloging-in-Publication Data

Sturm, Jeanne.
  Restoring wetlands / Jeanne Sturm.
     p. cm. -- (Let's explore science)
  ISBN 978-1-60694-409-7 (hard cover)
  ISBN 978-1-60694-527-8 (soft cover)
  1. Wetland restoration--Florida--Everglades--Juvenile literature. 2. Wetland restoration--California--Arcata Marsh and Wildlife Sanctuary--Juvenile literature. 3. Wetland ecology--Juvenile literature. 4. Bar-tailed godwit--Effect of habitat modification on--Juvenile literature. I. Title.

  QH76.5.F6 S78 2010
  333.95/28816--dc22

                    2009006081

Printed in the USA

CG/CG

www.rourkepublishing.com - rourke@rourkepublishing.com
Post Office Box 643328 Vero Beach, Florida 32964

Table of Contents

CHAPTER ONE

What are Wetlands?

Wetlands are **ecosystems** where water covers the soil, or is near the surface of the soil, for most or all of the year. You can find wetlands on every continent except Antarctica, from the tundra to the tropics.

Wetlands provide a habitat for a wide variety of plants and animals.

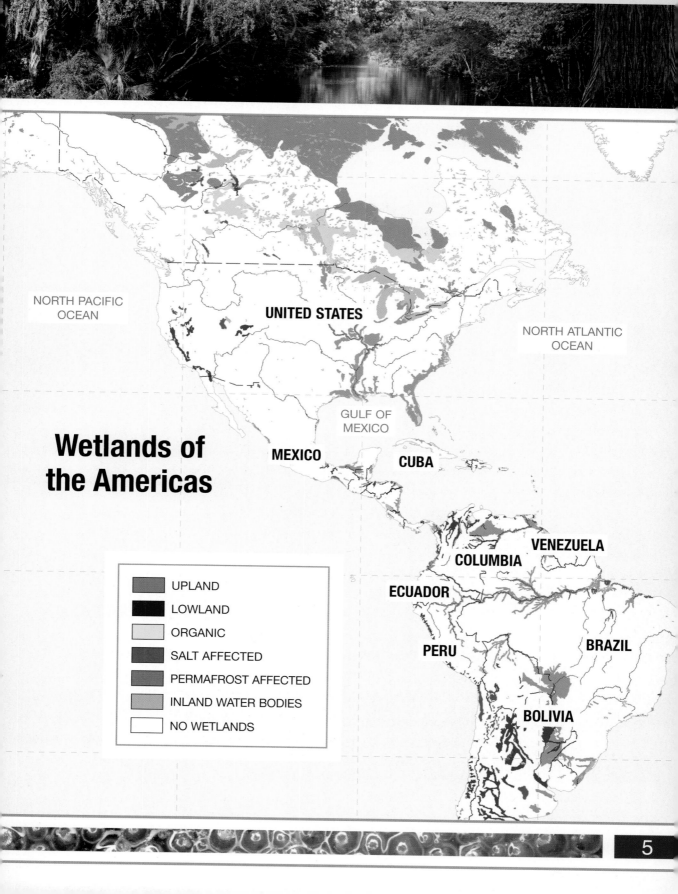

Wetlands of
the Americas

NORTH PACIFIC
OCEAN

UNITED STATES

NORTH ATLANTIC
OCEAN

GULF OF
MEXICO

MEXICO

CUBA

VENEZUELA

COLUMBIA

ECUADOR

PERU

BRAZIL

BOLIVIA

	UPLAND
	LOWLAND
	ORGANIC
	SALT AFFECTED
	PERMAFROST AFFECTED
	INLAND WATER BODIES
	NO WETLANDS

On North Carolina's Outer Banks, coastal marshes are home to waterfowl, fish, birds, mammals, and amphibians.

There are two general types of wetlands: coastal, sometimes called tidal, and inland. We find coastal wetlands near the ocean, where saltwater mixes with fresh water to form varying degrees of **brackish** water. In coastal wetlands, the water levels vary throughout the day due to the changing tides.

Few plants grow well under these conditions, so many shallow coastal wetlands are barren mud flats or sand flats. However, in some wetlands we can find grasses or mangroves that have adapted to the salty water.

Inland wetlands contain fresh water. They may be found along rivers and streams, near lakes and ponds, or off by themselves, surrounded by dry land.

In England, grasses growing along an estuary help small animals hide from their predators.

Permanent wetlands contain water year round, while seasonal wetlands are wet 6 months or less. Temporary wetlands contain water for only 30 days or less each year.

Wetlands in Colorado's Gunnison National Forest provide food and water to migratory birds.

CHAPTER TWO

The Importance of Wetlands

Wetlands are important to the Earth in many ways. They produce a great variety of grasses, trees, and flowers. Many of these plants provide food and shelter for the birds, amphibians, reptiles, and insects that live in the wetland year-round, as well as the migratory birds who use the wetlands for their breeding and resting grounds.

Many species of fish rely on **estuaries**, salt marshes, and coastal areas for their spawning grounds.

Reptiles, like the red-eared slider, are cold-blooded. They get their warmth from the Sun.

Blue herons make their nests in trees or bushes near water.

Rainbow trout are members of the salmon family. Adults weigh about
8 pounds (3.6 kilograms) on average, but can grow to as much as
53 pounds (24 kilograms).

Wetlands are important to the Earth's health. They act as **reservoirs** for runoff water during periods of heavy rain. When rain and snow sink into the ground, they are stored beneath the wetlands. This groundwater is an important source of drinking water, especially for people living far from lakes or rivers.

Wetlands also act as filters, removing **impurities** from the water that passes through them. As water moves through, the wetlands filter out excess nutrients and pollutants. These substances will eventually be absorbed by new living things.

Wetland plants are adapted to growing in wet soil with little oxygen.

DID YOU KNOW?

The St. Johns River is the longest northward-flowing river in the United States. At 310 miles (500 kilometers), it is the longest river in the state of Florida.

Many animals make their homes in and around the river. Alligators share the brackish waters with both freshwater and saltwater species of fish. Bald eagles and ospreys fly overhead. And in winter months, manatees take advantage of the warm water flowing from the river's natural springs.

Wetlands serve as a buffer when a hurricane, typhoon, or tsunami hits a coastal area. The mangrove forests that grow in wetland areas stabilize shorelines, protecting them from the waves and wind that accompany extreme weather.

DID YOU KNOW?

On December 26, 2004, a devastating tsunami struck southern Asia. In Sri Lanka, an island country off the coast of India, two villages came through the disaster with far different results. Only two people died in one of the villages, while almost 6,000 died in the other. The World Conservation Union credits mangrove forests with saving those lives. Mangroves, which grow in brackish coastal waters, protect the coastline from erosion, and can protect communities from typhoons, hurricanes, and tsunamis.

Researchers say healthy mangrove forests can absorb 30-40 percent of the destructive force of a tsunami. Since the 2004 disaster, mangrove forests are being restored in many coastal communities to protect against future tsunamis.

Wetlands are vital to the condition of our planet. They produce food and shelter for animals, filter and store water, protect shorelines from tropical storms,and reduce erosion from floodwaters.

Healthy coastal plants provide shelter for egrets.

Besides providing food for the many animals that live there, wetlands also provide great varieties of food for humans. Estuaries give us shellfish such as crabs, clams, oysters, and shrimp.

CHAPTER THREE

Animals of the Wetlands

Wetlands provide a home for a wide variety of animals. Amphibians, including salamanders, frogs, and toads, breed in the wetland habitat. Many species lay their eggs underwater. Others lay their eggs on the moist land nearby.

Fire salamanders are nocturnal. At night, they hunt for prey including insects, spiders, earthworms, and slugs.

The northern leopard frog lives near ponds and marshes, and, occasionally, grasslands. Leopard frogs eat ants, flies, worms, and beetles. Sometimes they will even eat birds, garter snakes, and other frogs.

Pollution and deforestation have led to a decline in the leopard frog population.

Every wetland has its share of insect life. Crane flies live in the mud and wet moss near streams and lakes. They provide food for many species of birds and fish.

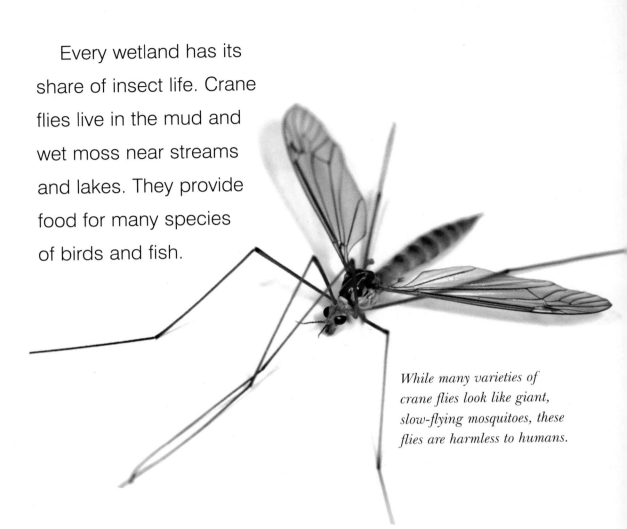

While many varieties of crane flies look like giant, slow-flying mosquitoes, these flies are harmless to humans.

Water striders, insects that live on the water's surface, use their short, front legs to catch small insects. They use their middle legs as paddles, and their back legs help them steer.

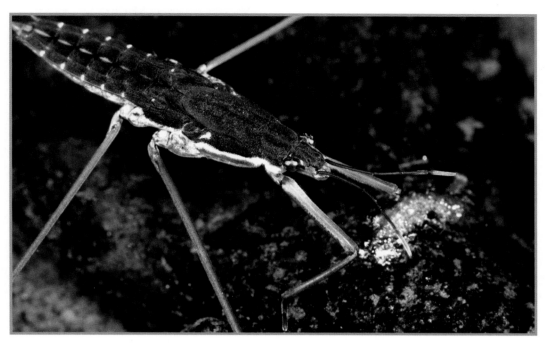

Water striders eat by sucking the body juices from their prey.

Whirligig beetles also live on the water's surface. They avoid predators by hanging out in groups. Thanks to their divided compound eyes, whirligig beetles can see above and below the water line at the same time.

Wetlands are nesting areas to many bird species, including pelicans, herons, egrets, and red-winged blackbirds. Great egrets build their nests in trees close to wetlands. They feed in shallow water, using their long, sharp bills to spear fish, frogs, or insects.

Egrets nest in colonies with other species of birds. They can lay anywhere from one to six eggs, but three is most common.

Egrets will feed in marshes, swamps, rivers, lakes, and even flooded fields.

The peregrine falcon eats songbirds, ducks, and even bats. Flying at great speeds, it uses its half-closed foot to stun or kill its prey in midair.

Migratory birds, such as whooping cranes and peregrine falcons, use wetlands as resting points during their migrations. They feed on the animals that live in and around the wetlands.

Some birds travel great distances when they migrate. One species, the bar-tailed godwit, migrates from Alaska to New Zealand each September and back again each March.

When the godwits migrate north in the spring, they stop to rest and eat in wetlands along the Yellow Sea. However, mudflats and marshes in the area have been drained to make way for development. As wetlands are drained, vital food sources for the birds are lost. Without this critical link in the migratory route, many godwits have been unable to make it back to their Alaskan breeding grounds.

From the 1990s to 2008, the number of bar-tailed godwits migrating to New Zealand dropped by more than half, from 155,000 down to 70,000.

DID YOU KNOW?

After adding large fat reserves to her body in Alaska, this bar-tailed godwit began her migration south, flying 7,145 miles (11,500 kilometers) to New Zealand without stopping even once. Though she did not eat or drink, the bird was able to sleep by shutting down one side of her brain at a time. For nourishment, she burned up the reserves of fat that she had put on in Alaska.

Scientists attached satellite transmitters to bar-tailed godwits so they could track the birds' migratory pattern.

RUSSIA

Alaska

CHINA

Yellow
Sea

PACIFIC OCEAN

AUSTRALIA

New Zealand

CHAPTER FOUR

The Destruction of Wetlands

Knowing what we do about the benefits of healthy wetlands, it's hard to imagine purposefully destroying them. Unfortunately, people didn't always understand the importance or usefulness of these marshes, swamps, and bogs.

When they encountered a wetland area, settlers saw mosquito breeding grounds and wet, mucky soil. On top of that, there was the smell; the unpleasant odor of **methane** released by organisms living in the soil.

Developers have drained many wetlands to make way for farmland, homes, and industrial complexes.

Still, others have been altered by **levees** and dams built to control flooding. The seasonal flooding, though, served a purpose. It nourished and enriched the soil in the wetlands. Because of the levees and dams, nutrient-rich sediments once deposited in wetlands are now carried far out into gulfs or oceans; their nutrients wasted.

DID YOU KNOW?

In 1849, 1850, and 1860, deeming wetlands a menace and a hindrance to land development, Congress passed a series of acts encouraging the draining and filling of wetlands. The first Swamp Land Act gave Louisiana the right to drain and fill all swamp and overflow lands. In 1850 and 1860, fourteen more states received the same authority. The idea was that the states could reclaim the land that in its current state seemed worthless and unprofitable. Since the passage of the Swamp Land Acts, more than half the wetlands in the United States have been destroyed.

CHAPTER FIVE

The Everglades: A Wetland in Crisis

The Florida Everglades wetland covers much of southern Florida. It is one of the largest wetlands in the world, a massive **watershed** that includes many different **habitats** that are home to plant and animal species found nowhere else on Earth.

The area below the yellow line is the Everglades ecosystem. It includes Lake Okeechobee, the Everglades, the Big Cypress Swamp, the Atlantic Coastal Ridge, the Florida Bay, and the Ten Thousand Islands estuaries.

Originally, the Everglades covered almost a third of the state of Florida. But in the early 1900s, settlers drained much of the water so that they could build homes and plant crops on the land. They channeled the water that flowed from Lake Okeechobee and built dams and **dikes** to control flooding. They never considered the impact of their changes on the existing ecosystem.

Canal locks manage the flow of water in the Everglades Drainage District.

By the time Floridians understood the value of the wetlands, they were already dependent on the water they obtained and the crops they harvested. But they were beginning to understand that the benefits they enjoyed came at a cost. Agricultural runoff polluted the waters, and plant and animal ecosystems were being destroyed. Formerly vibrant estuaries were empty, and **rookeries**, the breeding grounds of wading birds, were gone.

More than a dozen Everglades animals are now on the **endangered species** list, including the West Indian manatee, the Florida panther, and the American crocodile. The southern bald eagle and loggerhead turtle are just two of the animals listed as **threatened**.

Even though bald eagles are protected by federal and state laws, they face continuing threats from habitat loss, pesticides, and poisons.

Untreated wastewater pours into a stream, further polluting a water source for local animals.

CHAPTER SIX

Restoring the Everglades

Ms. Douglas spent the last decades of her life tirelessly working on behalf of the Everglades. She lived to the age of 108.

In 1991, the Florida legislature passed the Marjory Stoneman Douglas Everglades Protection Act, designed to restore the Everglades. One project of the plan is to build constructed, or man-made, wetlands. These artificial marshes will filter nutrients from agricultural runoff just as natural wetlands have always done, and they will supply clean water to the plants and animals living in the Everglades.

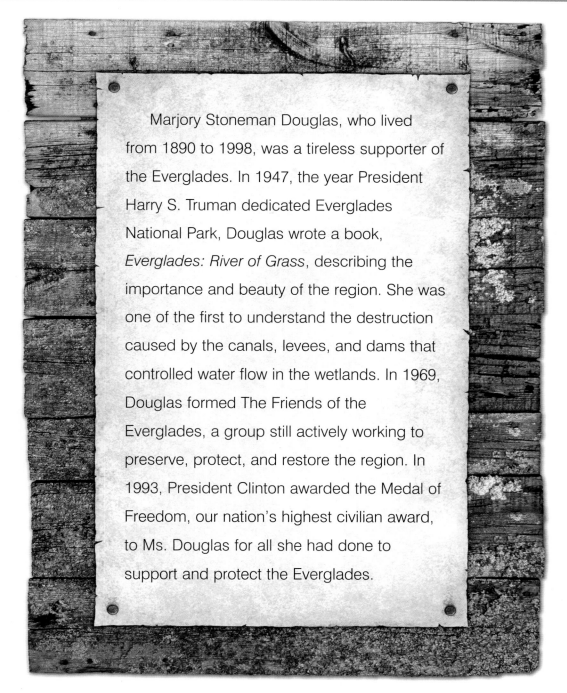

Marjory Stoneman Douglas, who lived from 1890 to 1998, was a tireless supporter of the Everglades. In 1947, the year President Harry S. Truman dedicated Everglades National Park, Douglas wrote a book, *Everglades: River of Grass*, describing the importance and beauty of the region. She was one of the first to understand the destruction caused by the canals, levees, and dams that controlled water flow in the wetlands. In 1969, Douglas formed The Friends of the Everglades, a group still actively working to preserve, protect, and restore the region. In 1993, President Clinton awarded the Medal of Freedom, our nation's highest civilian award, to Ms. Douglas for all she had done to support and protect the Everglades.

In 2000, scientists began working with government agencies to devise the Comprehensive Everglades Restoration Plan (CERP), a project designed to "restore, protect, and preserve the water resources of central and southern Florida, including the Everglades." The plan will redirect fresh water that now flows unused to the Atlantic Ocean and the Gulf of Mexico back to the marshes to hopefully reverse a century's worth of damage to the Everglades.

Environmental engineers survey wetlands and take soil samples to test for pollutants.

One of CERP's goals is to restore the clean water that provides a healthy habitat for Everglades wildlife.

The plan would restore the natural flow of water through the wetlands by removing hundreds of miles of man-made canals and levees. The state also plans to rebuild marshes so they can filter polluted water coming from farms and sugarcane fields.

The massive project includes many smaller projects, and the ultimate goal is a renewed ecosystem that can once again support healthy populations of fish, birds, alligators, and native plants.

CHAPTER SEVEN

The Arcata Marsh

The Arcata Marsh and Wildlife Sanctuary is a story of innovation and success. Up until the 1970s, the people of Arcata, California, along with other nearby towns, depended on outdated wastewater treatment systems that dumped raw sewage into nearby Humboldt Bay.

The Clean Water Act made it illegal to release untreated waste into the water.

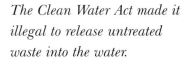

In 1972, Congress passed the Clean Water Act. The objective of the federal act was to restore the nation's waters by reducing pollution.

The state of California made plans to obey the Clean Water Act by building an expensive sewage treatment plant in Arcata, but residents resisted. The water treatment plant would be costly and it would take away from the natural beauty of the area.

The state told Arcata residents that if they did not want the water treatment plant built, they needed to come up with a plan of their own, but the wastewater that left their city must meet state water standards before it was discharged into the bay.

Arcata's creative solution was to rebuild nature. The city formed a plan to combine a sewage treatment plant with man-made marshes. Just as nature's wetlands filter pollutants out of water, these **constructed marshes** could clean the city's wastewater before it made its way to the bay.

Marsh plants thrive in the man-made wetland.

Workers reshaped the land, recovered the area with topsoil, and added water. Slowly, grasses and other plants began to grow, and the area began to look and act like a marsh.

CHAPTER EIGHT

The Arcata Marsh at Work

Water treatment in the constructed marsh begins when sewage flows into the collection area. Here, wastewater is separated from **sludge**. The sludge is treated and ultimately becomes compost to be used on the town's flowerbeds and forest floors.

The wastewater travels to an **oxidation** pond, where sunlight kills most of the **microbes**. It then flows into a series of marsh ponds and mixes with water from the bay.

Hairs that grow along the roots of marsh plants attract any remaining pollutants, and bacteria living near the roots break them down into harmless chemicals. Finally, the clean water makes its way into Humboldt Bay.

In an oxidation pond, brackish water from the bay meets treated wastewater.

As sludge settles out of the wastewater, the rotating arm atop the clarifying tank removes grease and soils.

Now, herons, snowy egrets, and pelicans live and feed along the marsh. Swallows take to the air, dining on mosquitoes. Nests are safely tucked away in bulrushes that grow in the shallow wetland. But plants and animals aren't the only ones who enjoy Arcata's constructed marsh. Since it opened, it has become a popular hiking, picnic, and fishing area for residents of the town. Locals, who fought to build the marsh, now enjoy its beauty year-round.

A heron spears its prey with a quick lunge of its bill. Herons eat a great variety of animals, including fish, amphibians, birds, and reptiles.

DID YOU KNOW?

Bill Giese, a wildlife manager, and Dr. Brian Needelman, a soil scientist at the University of Maryland, are part of a team intent on restoring marshes at the Blackwater National Wildlife Refuge in Maryland. One of their goals is to reduce carbon dioxide emissions that contribute to global warming. The team rebuilds wetlands by planting marsh grasses in soil pumped in from the bottom of rivers and bays. When marsh grasses die and decompose in the water, they take carbon dioxide out of the atmosphere. An acre of healthy marshland can remove 3 to 8 tons of carbon dioxide each year.

CHAPTER NINE

Is There Hope for the Bar-Tailed Godwit?

Wildlife that once struggled to survive now thrives in northern California's Arcata marsh. Can the bar-tailed godwit enjoy a similar success story? The species depends on the wetlands that surround the Yellow Sea, including the Saemangeum wetland in South Korea. Sadly, this wetland underwent a devastating change in 2006, when South Koreans completed a fifteen-year project to build a seawall along the wetland.

When it was completed, engineers drained the wetland, putting tens of thousands of migrating birds at risk of starvation, and affecting the livelihoods of 25,000 people from fishing communities along the coast of the Yellow Sea.

Godwits find their food in mudflats and marshes.

Too late, those who had built the seawall discovered there was not enough water to irrigate the crops they had planned to grow. And then, instead of making a decision to restore the wetland, they began discussing other possible uses of the land, including the building of a golf course or casino.

Meanwhile, at least two bird species face extinction, and shellfish, fish, and plants are stressed and dying.

There is a glimmer of hope, though. Engineers have placed sluice gates in the Saemangeum seawall. Sluice gates are wooden or metal plates that open and close to manage the flow of water. If the Korean government would allow the gates to be kept open, the tide would return, bringing food to the birds and the people who live along the wetland. Conservation groups are doing all they can to make it happen, which is good news for the people, plants, and animals of the Saemangeum wetland and the population of bar-tailed godwits that rely on it.

Wetlands are vital to a healthy planet. We can all do our part by keeping pollution out of wetlands and by teaching others how wetlands work to help the Earth.

GLOSSARY

brackish (BRAK-ish): slightly salty

constructed marshes (kuhn-STRUHKT-id MARSH-iz): man-made marshes, built to imitate nature

dikes (DIKES): walls or dams built to hold back water

ecosystems (EE-koh-sisstuhmz): communities of plants and animals living in their environments

endangered species (en-DAYN-jurd SPEE-sheez): a species of plant or animal that is in danger of extinction

estuaries (ESS-chu-er-eez): areas where rivers meet the sea

habitats (HAB-uh-tats): the natural environments of animals or plants

impurities (im-PYOOR-it-eez): foreign objects that contaminate a substance

levees (LEV-eez): areas built up to prevent flooding

methane (METH-ane): a gas released by bacteria when they decompose organic matter

microbes (MYE-krobez): germs that can cause disease

oxidation (ok-suh-DAY-shuhn): the process of being combined with oxygen

reservoirs (REZ-ur-vwarz): places where a large amount of water can be stored

rookeries (RUK-ur-eez): places where seabirds breed

sludge (SLUHJ): the solid matter of sewage when it is separated from the liquid

threatened (THRET-uhnd): a plant or animal at risk of becoming endangered

watershed (WAW-tur-shed): the land area that drains into a river or lake

wetlands (WET-landz): land where there is much moisture in the soil for all or part of the year

Index

Websites to Visit

www.epa.gov/OWOW/wetlands

www.geocities.com/ntgreencitizen/birdsandwetlands

www.sciencedaily.com

www.ecotippingpoints.org/ETP-Stories/indepth/usaarcata

About the Author

Jeanne Sturm grew up exploring the woods, waterfalls, and riverbanks around her home in Chagrin Falls, Ohio. She earned her education degree at Bowling Green State University and moved to Tampa, Florida, where she now lives with her husband, Kurt, and their three children.